AF269432

SWEDEN

R.L. Van

Big Buddy Books
An Imprint of Abdo Publishing
abdobooks.com

abdobooks.com

Published by Abdo Publishing, a division of ABDO, PO Box 398166, Minneapolis, Minnesota 55439.
Copyright © 2023 by Abdo Consulting Group, Inc. International copyrights reserved in all countries. No part of this book may be reproduced in any form without written permission from the publisher. Big Buddy Books™ is a trademark and logo of Abdo Publishing.

Printed in the United States of America, North Mankato, Minnesota
102022
012023

Design: Emily O'Malley, Mighty Media, Inc.
Production: Mighty Media, Inc.
Editor: Jessica Rusick
Cover Photograph: Mistervlad/Shutterstock Images
Interior Photographs: AlbertoGonzalez/Shutterstock Images, p. 15; Alexandros Michailidis/Shutterstock Images, p. 29 (top); almgren/Shutterstock Images, p. 17; Andrey Emelyanenko/Shutterstock Images, p. 13; Bengt Nyman/Wikimedia Commons, p. 29 (bottom); Globe Turner/Shutterstock Images, p. 30 (flag); IgorGolovniov/Shutterstock Images, p. 28 (top); Ingus Kruklitis/Shutterstock Images, p. 6 (bottom); Jeppe Gustafsson/Shutterstock Images, p. 26 (left); kimson/Shutterstock Images, p. 27 (top right); krivbass/Shutterstock Images, p. 6 (middle); lukulo/iStockphoto, pp. 5 (compass), 7 (compass); Mistervlad/Shutterstock Images, pp. 6 (top), 28 (bottom left); Mykola Klym/Shutterstock Images, p. 30 (currency); Paolo Bona/Shutterstock Images, p. 27 (bottom); Per Grunditz/Shutterstock Images, p. 23; Petr Kahanek/Shutterstock Images, p. 25; Piotr Wawrzyniuk/Shutterstock Images, p. 27 (top left); Pyty/Shutterstock Images, p. 5 (map); Rolf_52/Shutterstock Images, p. 9; Ruslan Maiborodin/Shutterstock Images, p. 7 (map); Sergii Koval/Shutterstock Images, p. 19; Trygve Finkelsen/Shutterstock Images, p. 26 (right); Wikimedia Commons, pp. 11, 21, 28 (bottom right)
Design Elements: Mighty Media, Inc.
Country population and area figures taken from the CIA World Factbook

Library of Congress Control Number: 2022940516

Publisher's Cataloging-in-Publication Data
Names: Van, R.L., author.
Title: Sweden / by R.L. Van
Description: Minneapolis, Minnesota : Abdo Publishing, 2023 | Series: Countries | Includes online resources and index.
Identifiers: ISBN 9781532199745 (lib. bdg.) | ISBN 9781098274948 (ebook)
Subjects: LCSH: Sweden--Juvenile literature. | Europe--Juvenile literature. | Scandinavia--Juvenile literature. | Sweden--History--Juvenile literature. | Geography--Juvenile literature.
Classification: DDC 948.5--dc23

CONTENTS

PASSPORT TO SWEDEN

Sweden is a country in Europe. It is on the **Scandinavian Peninsula**. It is bordered by two countries, the Baltic Sea, and the Gulf of Bothnia. More than 10.4 million people live there.

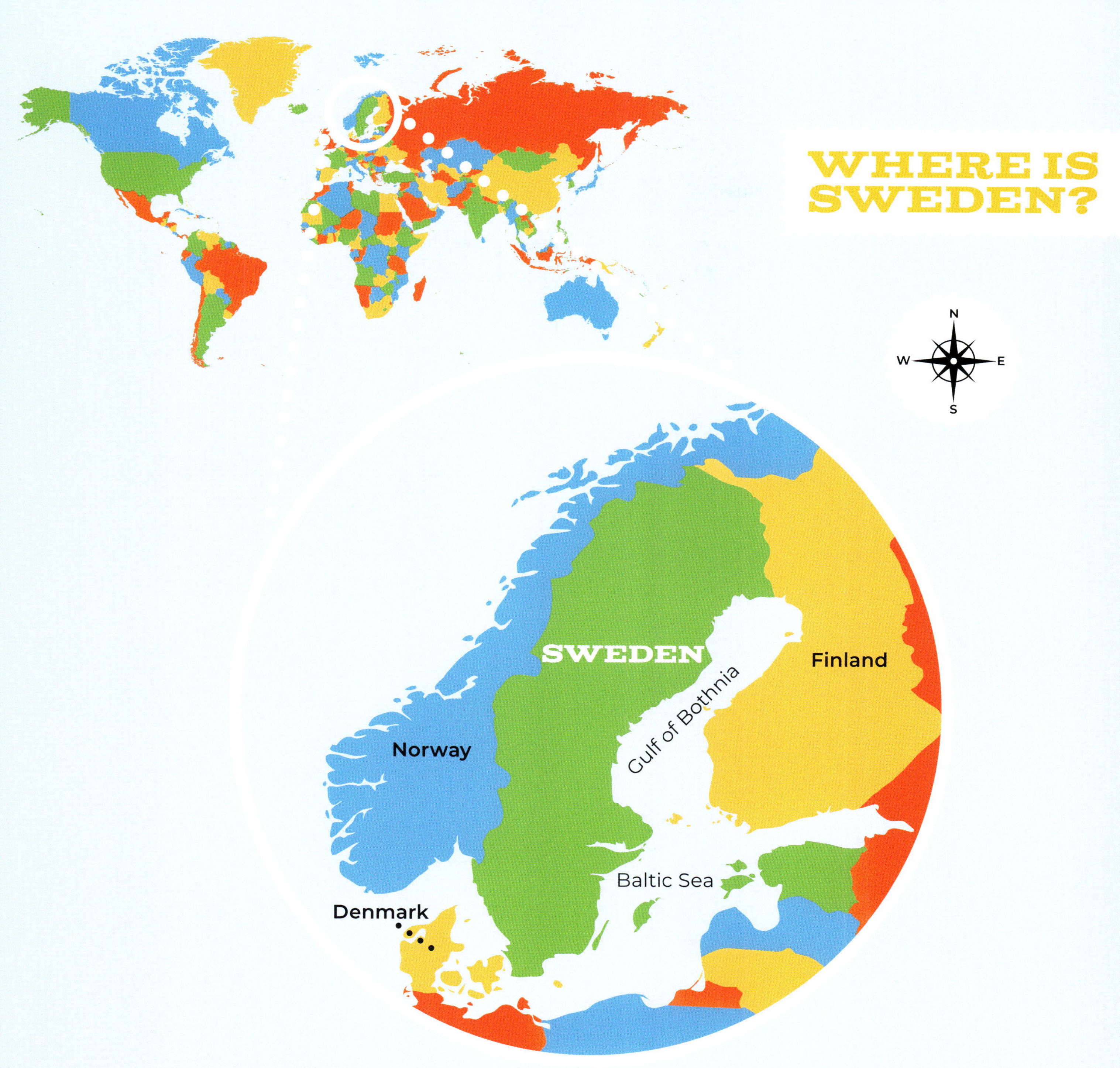

WHERE IS
SWEDEN?
N
W E
S
SWEDEN
Finland
Gulf of Bothnia
Norway
Baltic Sea
Denmark

IMPORTANT CITIES

Stockholm is Sweden's **capital** and largest city. It is a center of business, culture, education, and media.

Gothenburg is Sweden's second-largest city. It is home to Sweden's largest port. It is known for its seafood.

Malmö is Sweden's third-largest city. It is a diverse city with many parks and cycling paths.

SAY IT

Stockholm
STAHK-hohlm

Gothenburg
GOH-tun-brrgh

Malmö
MAHL-moh

DID YOU KNOW?

Malmö belonged to Denmark until 1658.

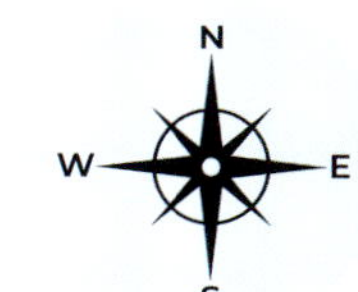

SWEDEN

Stockholm
Population: 1.66 million

Gothenburg
Population: 580,000

Malmö
Population: 351,749

SWEDEN IN HISTORY

Long ago, Sweden was covered by ice. As the area warmed, people settled the land. Beginning around 800, Viking tribes lived there. They traveled to nearby lands to trade goods. They often stole things and attacked people. In the 1100s, the different areas of Sweden **united**.

Gettlinge is a Viking burial ground in Sweden. Vikings arranged the stones in a boat shape to honor loved ones.

For many years, Sweden was **united** with other **Scandinavian** countries. It became independent in 1523. Sweden was strong in the 1600s. In the 1800s, the population grew. There was not enough land or work. Many people moved out of Sweden. By 1900, Sweden was an **industrial** country.

During the 1880s, nearly 330,000 people moved from Sweden to the United States.

AN IMPORTANT SYMBOL

Sweden's flag is blue with a yellow Nordic cross. The cross represents **Christianity**.

Sweden is a **parliamentary constitutional monarchy**. Parliament makes laws. The prime minister is head of government. The king or queen is head of state.

Most Scandinavian countries
have a Nordic cross on their flags.

ACROSS THE LAND

Sweden has mountains, coasts, **glaciers**, rivers, lakes, and forests. Moose, foxes, reindeer, lynx, and fish live in Sweden. Berries, wildflowers, mushrooms, and many types of trees grow there. Orchids grow on the islands of Gotland and Öland.

Lapland is Sweden's northernmost region. It is a popular spot to view the northern lights.

EARNING A LIVING

Factory workers in Sweden make cars, medicines, and machinery. Many people have service jobs, such as working for the government.

Sweden's **natural resources** include timber, gold, copper, and zinc. Farmers produce sugar beets, grains, potatoes, milk, and meat.

Most Swedish farms are in the south of the country. The growing season is longer there.

LIFE IN SWEDEN

Most Swedish people live in cities. They eat pickled foods, fish, meatballs, sausage, potatoes, berries, and sweet rolls. Soccer, ice hockey, golf, and gymnastics are popular sports. Many Swedish people also enjoy hiking and skiing.

Meatballs, lingonberries, and mashed potatoes is a classic Swedish meal.

FAMOUS FACES

Alfred Nobel was born on October 21, 1833, in Stockholm. He was a scientist and businessman who invented dynamite. When he died in 1896, Nobel left money to start the Nobel Prizes. Today, these prizes are given each year to people whose work has helped the world.

Alfred Nobel held 355 patents for different inventions.

Greta Thunberg was born in Stockholm. In 2018, at age 15, she began speaking out against climate change. Her work inspired many other young people to fight for climate action. Thunberg was named *Time* magazine's Person of the Year in 2019.

Greta Thunberg has given many speeches on climate change before world leaders.

A GREAT COUNTRY

Sweden has beautiful land and a rich history and culture. The people and places of Sweden help make the world a more interesting place.

Sweden's Sarek National Park is the oldest in Europe. It was established in 1909.

TOUR BOOK

LEARN

Visit ABBA The Museum in Stockholm to learn about this famous musical group.

PLAY

Spend the day at Liseberg in Gothenburg. It is **Scandinavia's** biggest amusement park.

DANCE

Celebrate Midsummer. Every June, people dance around decorated poles for this holiday.

SEE

Wander the streets of Malmö in search of tiny mouse-themed miniatures. They are created by a group called Anonymouse.

EXPLORE

Visit Astrid Lindgren's World in Vimmerby. This theater and park has characters from Lindgren's books, such as *Pippi Longstocking*.

TIMELINE

1397

The Kalmar Union began. Sweden, Norway, and Denmark **united** under one ruler.

1611

Gustavus Adolphus became king. He helped Sweden become powerful.

1436

Stockholm became Sweden's **capital**.

1901

The first Nobel Prizes were awarded. These were named for Swedish inventor Alfred Nobel.

1974

The Swedish music group ABBA won the Eurovision Song Contest. They became famous around the world.

2021

Magdalena Andersson became Sweden's first female prime minister.

2012

Princess Estelle was born. She became second in line to the Swedish throne.

SWEDEN
UP CLOSE

Official Name
Konungariket Sverige
(Kingdom of Sweden)

Flag

Population
10,483,647 (2022 est.)
89th-most-populated country

Total Area
173,860 square miles
(450,295 sq km)
55th-largest country

Official Language
Swedish

Capital
Stockholm

Currency
Swedish krona

Form of Government
Parliamentary
constitutional
monarchy

National Anthem
"Du Gamla, Du Fria"
("Thou Ancient,
Thou Free")

GLOSSARY

capital—a city where government leaders meet.

Christianity—a religion based on the teachings of Jesus Christ.

glacier (GLAY-shuhr)—a huge chunk of ice and snow on land.

industrial—relating to the organized action of making goods and services for sale.

natural resources—useful and valuable supplies from nature.

parliamentary constitutional monarchy—a form of government in which a parliament makes the laws. The king or queen has only those powers given by a country's laws and constitution.

peninsula—a stretch of land coming out from a mainland and almost entirely surrounded by water.

Scandinavian (skan-duh-NAY-vee-uhn)—of or relating to the people, languages, or life in the countries of Sweden, Denmark, and Norway. The countries are together known as Scandinavia.

unite—to come together for a purpose or action.

ONLINE RESOURCES

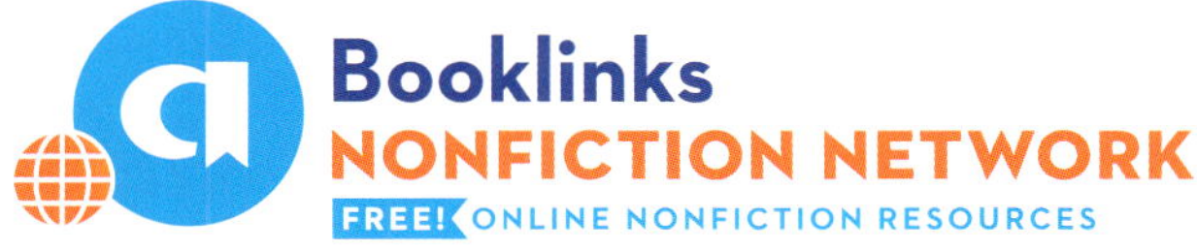

To learn more about Sweden, please visit **abdobooklinks.com** or scan this QR code. These links are routinely monitored and updated to provide the most current information available.

INDEX